STORY TIME THREE

STORY TIME
THREE

Jeanne Wesson

Illustrated by
Donald Grey

SCRIPTURE UNION
5 Wigmore Street, London W1H OAD

© Scripture Union 1968

First published 1968

Reprinted 1972

Reprinted 1973

ISBN 0 85421 183 7

Printed in Malta by St Paul's Press Ltd

Contents

Contents

God's World

This is the world that God built.

But once, in God's time, there was nothing. Nothing at all. No morning, no night, no earth and no sky. No sea, no beach, no trees, no flowers and no vegetables.

No sun, no moon and no stars. No birds and no fish.

Not even one small animal to play with. Not even one Mummy, one Daddy or one baby. Nothing at all.

7

If *you* want to know what this nothing was like, shut your eyes very tight. Now, you can *see* nothing. That's what it was like.

Then God began to build something in the nothing.

He created the morning to get up in and the night for going to bed. He created the earth that you dance and skip and jump on and the sky in which aeroplanes fly.

He made the sea that the ships sail on. He made earth for you to dig, trees for you to sit under in the summer, flowers to pick and vegetables to eat.

In the morning you sometimes see the sun that keeps us warm. God made the sun. At bedtime, you may see the big, shining moon and the little twinkling stars. God made those too.

He created all the birds in the trees, the greedy fat pigeons and the tiny little sparrows.

He created the fishes in the ponds; the red gold fish and the quick stickleback.

He created the animals on the farm; the cows that say 'Moo,' and the sheep that go 'Baa.'

9

He created the animals you see at the zoo; the sad, humpy camel that used to live in the desert sands and the mischievous monkey that swung on the jungle trees. But best of all He made families. Families with black cheeks, and brown cheeks and yellow cheeks and pink cheeks, to live in the world that He built. He made Daddys and Mummys, boys and girls and babies. He planned that they should love one another.

10

A Prayer

Thank You, God, for all the lovely things You made, especially the . . . (Think of all the things you would like to say thank you for.)

One man obeys God

Noah was his name . . . Mr. Noah. There was Mrs. Noah too, and one little, two little, three little boys. God loved them all, and they were good people who did as He told them to do. So, one day, when God told Mr. Noah to build a very large boat indeed, he began to do so even though there was not a pond, a lake or sea to sail it on. He didn't say 'I don't want to,' or 'No' or 'I shan't!' He got on with it, just like that.

God told Mr. Noah that the boat was to be very long and very tall and very big. So big that he and Mrs. Noah and the one, two, three boys would be able to live in it. The one, two, three boys were no longer little, but had grown into men and each had a wife of his own. God told Mr. Noah that the boat should be big enough to give many animals a home there too. So big that Mr. Noah would have room for an enormous store cupboard in which to store food for himself, food for his family and food for the animals

12

So Mr. Noah built his boat. He made it very long, and very tall and very big. It was big enough for Mr. Noah and Mrs. Noah. It was big enough for Mr. Noah's three sons and their three wives. It was big enough for many animals. It was big enough for an enormous store cupboard.

Then God told Mr. Noah to go and live in the big boat. So he did. So did Mrs. Noah and Mr. Noah's three sons and their three wives. They took with them two of every animal they could find. What animals do *you* think they found?

Of course Mr. Noah made sure that the enormous store cupboard was filled with every sort of food.

Then it began to rain. Not a few rain drops

but a great big storm that didn't stop. Rain, rain and still more rain. First of all, there were puddles on the earth, then the puddles became ponds, and the ponds became lakes and the lakes became a great, enormous sea. And on this sea Mr. Noah's boat began to sail. Every day Mr. Noah and the boys fed the animals from the enormous store cupboard. Every day Mrs. Noah and the wives prepared meals from the food in the enormous store cupboard. Every day God cared for them all, so they were safe and happy.

The rain didn't stop for a very long time. For days and days and days it went on raining. But one day the sun came out, and a dry wind began to blow. It blew and blew and blew. Slowly the sea became a lake again, the lake became a pond again, the pond became a puddle again and the big boat sat down on the earth.

Then God told Mr. Noah to get out of the boat. So he did. So did Mrs. Noah and Mr. Noah's three sons and their three wives. So did the animals. They pranced and they ran, and they rolled about. They were home on earth again. But they didn't know *why*. They didn't know what Mr. Noah knew and what you and I know. They didn't know that Mr.

16

Noah had done just what God told him to do. They didn't know that that was why he was safe and happy. But we do.

A Prayer

Thank You, God, for looking after me and my family. Help us all to do as You wish. Amen.

17

Uncle Abraham's home

Uncle Abraham lived in a very grand town-house. It was full of comfortable furniture and beautiful things. Uncle Abraham had every-
18

thing he wanted. Also, he loved God. Because he loved God, he liked to do whatever God told him to do.

One day, God told Uncle Abraham to leave his very grand town-house. God told him to go and live in a tent. This wouldn't be nearly so comfortable. But Uncle Abraham and Aunt Sarah, with all their helpers and friends, left their town-houses—which was a very obedient thing to do. They took all their camels, their cows and every animal. Also their money, their food, and their pots and pans. They went to live in tents instead. God wanted them to travel to a new country where he would give them a new home.

Lot went too. Uncle Abraham was his Uncle; that is why he went. All *his* helpers and friends went with him. They took all *their* camels, *their* cows and every animal. Also *their* money, *their* food and *their* pots and pans. They all went to live in tents, too.

To begin with, everyone was very happy together.

Then, one day, the men looking after Uncle Abraham's cows saw a long stretch of green, juicy grass.

'We'll take Uncle Abraham's cows there,' they said. So they did.

Then the men looking after Lot's cows saw the long stretch of green, juicy grass.

'We'll take Lot's cows there,' they said. So they did.

What a lot of fuss there was then! The men began to shout at one another.

'There's no room for *you*.'

'We got here first!'

'No, you didn't! We did!'

'Anyway, Uncle Abraham is the elder. His cows should have this grass.'

'No, they shouldn't!'

On and on and on it went. These quarrels made Uncle Abraham and Lot unhappy. So Uncle Abraham wondered what he could do about it. He thought and he thought. 'We can't stay together if my men are going to quarrel with Lot's men,' he said. 'We shall have to place our tents on different land.'

He called Lot to him. 'You can choose land where you would like your tents to be,' he said. 'I'll go somewhere else.' Lot didn't seem to notice how kind Uncle Abraham was.

Lot stood and looked at the land. First of all he looked one way. The grass looked dry and dirty that way. He didn't think his cows would enjoy *that* grass for their dinner. Then he looked the other way. The grass looked green and juicy. His cows would certainly enjoy *this* grass for their dinner. 'This is the best. I want this side. This is the best,' he thought.

Lot didn't think of Uncle Abraham at all. He was selfish and chose the best for himself.

But it was God who knew *all* about Uncle Abraham's men and Lot's men. It was God who knew how kind Uncle Abraham had been

and how selfish Lot had been. God was pleased with the way Abraham behaved. God called Abraham His friend.

A Prayer

Dear Heavenly Father, please help me to obey You. Help me to be as kind as Uncle Abraham was. Amen.

A favourite son

It was a lovely coat. The sort of coat Joseph had always wanted. It was bright and new looking and it had long warm sleeves. It was really the sleeves that started all the fuss. You see, they were so long, that they hung in the way if there was work to be done. So Joseph didn't *do* any work and all his brothers did. *They* went into the fields, *they* looked after the sheep. They could roll up their sleeves, so *they* did all the dirty work.

The brothers used to sit and grumble about it.

'It isn't fair,' one would say. 'Why should Father give Joseph such a splendid coat?'

'It isn't fair,' another would say. 'After all, he's a lot younger than we are.'

'It isn't fair,' another would say. 'He stays at home and we do all the work.'

'It isn't fair,' they grumbled. 'Father likes him better than all of us.'

And it was true. Father did. He *did* like Joseph better than all the others. That *was* why he gave Joseph such a magnificent coat.

One fine day, when Joseph was wearing his coat, his father spoke to him.

'Joseph,' he said. 'I want you to do something for me. Your brothers are looking after the sheep a long way from here. Please go and ask them how they are, for they've been away for a long time.'

So Joseph set off. He walked up the hills and down again, he climbed over rocks and he crossed the little streams until, at last, he saw his brothers.

They saw him coming, too! You'll remember that they were always grumbling about him. This day, they grumbled just the same, only as they grumbled a wicked idea came into their minds. They thought what fun it would be to pull Joseph's coat off him — his new-looking coat with the long, warm sleeves. They thought what fun it would be to frighten him by pushing him into a big hole on the hillside, a hole so big that he couldn't climb out of it. The strange thing was that they forgot about God. They forgot that God looks after people! They forgot that *He* would look after Joseph even if they didn't.

So the brothers pulled off Joseph's coat and they pushed him into the big hole on the

hillside and God knew all about it and understood how miserable Joseph felt.

After a while, the brothers looked up. Far away, on the line where the sky seemed to meet the green grass, there were some camels. Flummpity-flomp, flummpity-flomp went their great padded feet as they came nearer. The brothers saw that there were men riding on them. Rich, important men on their way to Egypt-land.

'Let's sell our Joseph to them,' shouted one of the brothers excitedly. The other brothers, who were always grumbling about Joseph

anyway, nodded. Quickly, and without his new-looking coat with the long warm sleeves, Joseph was pulled out of the big hole on the hillside, and sold to the rich important men, who bought him for twenty pieces of silver, and took him to Egypt-land. There they sold him to a kind man named Potiphar. Joseph was very happy working in Potiphar's house and God knew this. Although Joseph couldn't see Him, God was with him all the while.

A Prayer

Dear God, thank You for caring for me even when other people don't. Amen.

Joseph's job

Joseph was very happy. He enjoyed the work he had to do in Potiphar's house. God was looking after him and helping him to do everything very well.

'Well done,' Potiphar would say. 'I like the way you did that.'

'You have been busy today,' Potiphar would say, 'How nice everything looks.' Then the day came when Potiphar said, 'Because you do your work so well, I'm going to give you something more important to do for me.'

How proud Joseph felt! God was still looking after him and God helped him to do the more important work well, too. So Potiphar gave him some more important work, and then more important work and then more important work until Joseph became the most important person in Potiphar's house apart from Potiphar himself.

Joseph told all the other servants what to do. Joseph looked after Potiphar's money. Joseph

looked after Potiphar's house. Joseph looked after all the land that belonged to Potiphar, and all the things that grew in it and all the animals that fed on it. Yes, Joseph was very important indeed.

Then, one day, Potiphar's wife asked Joseph to do something that she knew Potiphar wouldn't like. Joseph knew this too and so he very bravely said 'No, I won't' and went away. Potiphar's wife asked him again and again and again. It wasn't easy to say 'No.' You have to be brave to say 'No' to wrong

things, but Joseph knew that God was helping him to be brave.

'No,' he said. 'I won't,' he said. 'Potiphar trusts me,' he said.

Potiphar's wife was cross, exceedingly cross. So cross that she told stories about Joseph that were not true — she made them up. She told them to Potiphar and he believed them. Then Potiphar was cross, so cross that he had Joseph taken from his house and put in a prison-house with a lot of wicked people who had done very wrong things.

Joseph was sad and miserable. He was not important now. He was an ordinary prisoner, but he was not quite the same as all the other men in that prison-house, for God was taking care of him.

When the man in charge of the prison saw Joseph he thought, H'm. He's a nice-looking boy.' Another day he thought, 'He doesn't look cruel like some of the men here.' Another day he thought, 'He doesn't say nasty things like some of the men here do.' Another day he thought, 'I think I could trust him.'

So he asked Joseph to do some work for him. God was still looking after Joseph and helped him to do the new work well. Soon . . . can you guess what happened? Joseph became the most important prisoner in the prison.

A Prayer

Heavenly Father, please help me to do things well, like Joseph did. Amen.

34

Pharaoh's bad day

Slowly, Pharaoh got out of bed. He was a lucky man. He was very important, he had a great deal of money; he had many servants and everyone in Egypt-land had to obey him. But today, he wasn't happy. He dressed very slowly. Then he played with the breakfast on

his plate instead of eating it.

'Perhaps he isn't feeling very well,' whispered his servants to one another.

Then Pharaoh spoke. 'Fetch me all the wise and clever men in Egypt-land,' he said. Soon they began to come to Pharaoh's palace. Fat ones and thin ones, tall ones and short ones, old and young . . . all of them very wise and very clever.

'I've had a dream,' said Pharaoh.

'So that's what it's all about,' whispered Pharaoh's servants to one another.

'I dreamt about some cows,' said Pharaoh and told the wise and clever men all about the dream.

'Then I had another dream,' said Pharaoh.

'Fancy that!' whispered his servants to one another.

'My second dream was about some corn growing in a field,' said Pharaoh and told the wise and clever men all about it. Everyone listened, but when Pharaoh had finished, no one said anything. They all sat very quietly and thought about the dreams. They couldn't think of anything helpful to say.

'He still looks unhappy,' whispered Pharaoh's servants to one another. Then, suddenly, one of Pharaoh's chief servants

boldly said, 'I think I know someone who can *really* help you.'

'Fancy that!' whispered all the other servants once again.

'When you put me in prison,' continued the chief servant, 'there was a young man there who helped me. I think he could help you, too. His name is Joseph.'

'Send for him at once,' commanded Pharaoh. So Joseph, who just now didn't look very wise or very clever, came to Pharaoh's palace.

'I've had two dreams,' said Pharaoh. 'I'm very worried about them. Perhaps you can help me.'

'I can't, but God can,' replied Joseph. 'God will help you by using me to help you.'

'How is God going to help?' whispered Pharaoh's servants to one another.

So Pharaoh told Joseph all about the cows and all about the corn which he had seen in his dreams. Then God helped Pharaoh, because Joseph was able to tell Pharaoh that the dreams were good dreams, not bad dreams. Joseph was able to pass on God's messages to Pharaoh. God helped him to be very wise.

Then Pharaoh smiled again.

'Oh, good!' whispered all his servants to one another.

Then Pharaoh took a gold ring off his own finger and put it on Joseph's. He gave Joseph beautiful clothes to wear and hung a gold chain round his neck. 'I am the most important person in Egypt-land', he said, 'but *you* shall be the next.'

'Well, well, well . . .' thought Pharaoh's servants and they all bowed to Joseph.

A Prayer

Dear God, please help me to help other people like Joseph did, especially . . . (Think of some people you may be able to help.)

The baby in the water-weeds

Mrs. Levi was nursing her baby. He gurgled and cooed and spluttered like happy babies do. Mrs. Levi loved her baby very much. She knew that God had given him to her and she looked after him very carefully — in the same way as she had looked after his brother Aaron and his sister Miriam, when they had been babies. They loved their new baby brother and helped Mrs. Levi look after him.

Mrs. Levi's baby would have grown up like all babies do, if it hadn't been for Mr. Pharaoh. He was the most important person in Egypt-land, and he didn't like the Hebrew people one little bit, and Mrs. Levi was a Hebrew. Mr. Pharaoh hated the Hebrew people so much that he said he would not have any more Hebrew baby boys in *his* Egypt-land.

Poor Mrs. Levi! She realized she must not let Mr. Pharaoh know about *her* baby. She dare not take the baby out in case someone SAW him and told Mr. Pharaoh. Every time

he cried, she ran and picked him up and rocked him in her arms till he stopped, in case someone HEARD him and told Mr. Pharaoh. And every day her baby grew bigger and bigger and his crying became noisier and noisier. At last the time came when Mrs. Levi could hide him no longer.

It was then that God gave her an idea.

This is what she did. She made a little basket. It was just big enough to put her baby in with all his covers. Then she wrapped her baby up warmly and placed him in the basket. Then she placed a lid on the basket which was rather like a pram canopy, only it had holes in it so that the baby could breathe the fresh air he needed. Then she and Miriam ran quickly out of the house down to the river. There, Mrs. Levi found a bush made of tall water-weeds. Carefully, she placed her precious basket in the centre of the weeds. It was a strong basket and her baby was very snug and safe and cosy inside.

'You stay,' she said to Miriam. 'Hide behind that tree and see what happens. I'd better go home before anyone sees me.' So off Mrs. Levi went.

It wasn't long before Mr. Pharaoh's daughter came down to the river to swim. She soon saw the basket in the water-weeds and wondered what it was, so she sent a girl to fetch it. There, inside the basket, she saw Mrs. Levi's little baby. He began to cry like babies do when they are hungry. 'Oh, dear!' she thought. 'Poor little baby!' She felt very sorry for him, and at that moment wished she could help him and make him happy.

When Miriam saw this she came out from
behind the tree where she had been hiding.
'Shall I find someone who can look after him
for you? Someone who can feed him and
make him happy?' she said.

'Yes, please,' said Mr. Pharaoh's daughter
who didn't want to hear him cry much longer.

So Miriam ran home and fetched Mrs. Levi.
'Come quickly,' she said. And, of course,
Mrs. Levi came at once.

'Please will you look after this baby for me?'
asked Pharaoh's daughter. 'I'm looking for
someone to feed him and make him happy.'

Mrs. Levi said that she would. How happy she was to have her own little baby in her arms once again! She knew that he was quite safe now, and said thank You to God for giving her the idea of putting him in that little basket. But it was Pharaoh's daughter who gave him a name. She decided to call him Moses.

A Prayer

Thank You, God, for helping Mrs. Levi to take care of her baby and to keep him safe. Please help my Mummy and Daddy to take care of me. Amen.

Ruth helps out

'It's been a super holiday,' said Peter. Peter and Dot were staying on a farm but tomorrow morning they were going home. Now they were with their Mother and Father watching the cows being led in for milking.

'*I'm* glad we're going home in the morning', said Mummy. 'I'm beginning to miss home now.'

'You are just like Naomi,' said Daddy, sitting down under a large oak tree. He patted the

ground. 'Come on! Sit down and I'll tell you all about her.' Peter and Dot flopped on to the grass beside him, then Mummy sat down, too.

'Naomi was old, as old as a granny,' said Daddy, 'and she had been away from her home for a very long time.'

'How long is a long time?' asked Dot.

'Longer than you can even remember!.' Daddy replied.

'Naomi lived in a house with Ruth and Orpah. One day she thought, "I'm beginning to miss my home now. I think I'll go back." So she called Ruth and she called Orpah. "I'm going back to my home now," she said. She knew she would have to walk home because there were no trains, or buses, or cars, or even bicycles.

'Now, Ruth loved Naomi and, best of all, she loved God, so she gave Naomi a big hug and kissed her, saying:

"I will go wherever you go;

I will live wherever you live;

Your friends shall be my friends;

Your God shall be my God."

But Orpah decided to stay.

'So Ruth went back with Naomi to her house. Naomi had been away so long that there was no food in the cupboard.'

'Did Ruth have to go to the supermarket?'
asked Peter.

'There were no supermarkets and no shops,'
said Daddy. 'People had to grow their own
food, so Ruth went down to the fields and
collected some corn so that Naomi could
bake bread for them to eat.'

Dot looked puzzled. 'Didn't the farmer
mind?'

'No,' said Daddy. 'You see God helped

51

Ruth to find a field belonging to a kind farmer. His name was Farmer Boaz. He let her pick up the corn from the edges of his fields. He even had a secret arrangement with the farmhands who worked for him. He told them to leave some good corn in the field so that Ruth would find it and take it home.'

'Was Naomi happy to be at home again?' asked Peter.

'Very happy,' said Daddy. 'You see, Ruth was a great help to her. Every day she went to the fields and every day she got to know Farmer Boaz better and better until, one day, he asked her to marry him. Some time later they had a little baby boy. Naomi was so happy to be a real Granny. She knew that God had looked after her and her family.'

Dot sighed. She put her arms round her Mummy's neck and gave her a hug. 'I love *you*,' she said. 'I think God looks after *our* family, too.'

A Prayer

Dear Father God, thank You for looking after our family. Amen.

Hannah's baby

Hannah so wanted a little baby. She wanted one very much indeed, but God had never sent her a baby of her own, so she was sad. Sometimes Hannah would cry because she was so sad. Most of her friends had little babies to look after and love; if only God would let her have one, too.

Mr. Elkanah was to have been her baby's Daddy. He was always very kind to Hannah, for he didn't like to see her looking so sad. He tried to cheer her up. 'Aren't I someone very special for you to love and look after?' he asked. Hannah smiled. She did love Mr. Elkanah very much, but she had love enough for him and for a little baby, too. Loving *just* Mr. Elkanah wasn't the same as having a little baby of their own for them *both* to look after.

One day they were going up to the Temple Church. Hannah liked to go to the church and talk to God there, but she didn't much like

seeing all the other ladies who had babies of their own. There was one lady she didn't like at all. Her name was Peninnah.

Peninnah always laughed at Hannah because she had no baby, and that was very unkind of her. On this day, Peninnah was just the same as she always was. If anything, she was worse! She was very rude to Hannah. Of course, this made Hannah feel sadder than ever.

Hannah knew that God was the only Person who could really help her. She knew that He could see that she had a baby if He wished to do so. Hannah left the others and went back to the Temple Church alone. She went in, knelt down, and began to talk to God. She told Him everything. She felt so sad and unhappy again that she began to cry.

'Please, God, give me a baby. A baby of my own,' she said. 'If You do, I'll see that he becomes a special helper in this Temple Church just as soon as he is old enough. He shall serve You always.'

Hannah knew that God was listening, for she had always been told that He listened to all the prayers of the people who love Him. What Hannah didn't know was that someone else was listening too! The minister of that Temple Church had been watching Hannah. Slowly, because he was old and found it difficult to walk, he came towards her.

'Don't be sad any more,' he said. 'I'm sure God will answer your prayer.'

Hannah was very happy when she left the church. She was even happier later on, for she and Mr. Elkanah had a small baby of their

very own. God gave them a baby boy which was just what Hannah had always wanted. Mr. Elkanah and Hannah were very proud of him and called him Samuel.

As the days went by, Samuel grew into a strong boy. When he was old enough to leave his mother without being unhappy, Hannah took him to the Temple Church so that he could help the Minister there — just as she had promised she would. She still loved him very much and used to visit him

there. When she did so, she always took him a new little coat to wear.

A Prayer

Thank You for listening to me when I talk to You, dear God. Please do what is best for me. Amen.

Samuel at night-time

'Mummy! MUMMY!' baby Samuel called. It was night-time and he had woken up. His Mummy soon came. She gave him a cuddle, tucked him in his bed again and he dropped off to sleep.

When Samuel grew into a big boy, he didn't mind waking up in the night. He didn't need to call his Mummy any more. He lived in the Temple Church and helped old Eli, the Minister. Eli had enjoyed a great many birthdays, and his body was getting tired and didn't work as well as it had when he was young. His legs were tired, so he always walked very slowly. His eyes were tired, so he didn't always see everything. He was pleased to have Samuel to help him. 'Samuel,' he would call, 'please do this.' 'Samuel,' he would call, 'please do that.'

One night, Samuel had just gone to bed. He lay down, pulled the covers up to his ears and closed his eyes. He was nearly asleep when . . .

'Samuel!' Samuel sat up and rubbed his eyes. 'Samuel!' he heard again. 'Eli is calling me,' he thought. Up he jumped and ran in to Eli. 'Here I am,' he said. 'Here I am, you called me.'

'No, I didn't call you,' said Eli. 'You go and lie down again.'

So Samuel went back to bed. He lay down, pulled the covers up to his ears and closed his eyes. He was nearly asleep when . . .

'Samuel! Samuel!' He heard the call again. Up he jumped and ran in to Eli. 'Here I am,' he said 'You called me.'

'No, I didn't call you,' said Eli for the second time. 'You go and lie down again.'

So Samuel went back to bed again. He lay down, pulled the covers up to his ears and closed his eyes. He was nearly asleep when . . .

'Samuel! Samuel!' He had heard the call once more. Up he jumped and ran in to Eli. 'Here I am,' he said. 'For you *did* call me.' 'Samuel,' Eli said, 'I didn't call you. I think *God* must be calling you. You go and lie down again. If God calls you again, say "Talk to me, Lord, for I am listening to You."'

So Samuel went back to bed. He lay down, pulled the covers up to his ears and listened.

'Samuel! Samuel!' There was Someone calling him again.

Samuel sat up. 'Talk to me, Lord, for I'm listening to You,' he said.

Then God did a very wonderful thing. He talked to Samuel and Samuel listened very carefully to everything He said. And ever after that Samuel loved God in a very special way.

A Prayer

Dear Heavenly Father, help me to love You as much as Samuel did. Amen.

David did

One, two, three, whee – ee – ee plomp. One, two, three, whee – ee – ee plomp. David grinned. The sheep went on munching the grass. David bent over, picked up a stone and put it in his sling. Then he swung his arm as though he were pretending to be a windmill, one, two, three times. Whee – ee – ee went this stone, then plomp! It landed by David's picnic lunch. So did the next stone, and the next, and the next.

David was a good shot. He wasn't old enough to join the army and fight in battles like his three big brothers, but he could hit any wild animal who came after *his* sheep.

Then David sat down and sang a little song to himself. He liked songs and he liked singing. Sometimes David made up his own songs; songs about birds and trees and streams and hills and wild animals. Sometimes David's songs were 'thank You' songs that he sang to God.

One day, David's father called to him. 'David,' he said, 'I want you to go and see your three brothers. Find out how they are and take fresh food for them to eat.'

So, next morning David asked someone else to look after his sheep. Then he set off to find his brothers. He was just saying 'hallo' to them when a strange thing happened.

Down by the river stood an enormous man. David had never seen such an enormous man before. He was tall and big and looked very tough indeed. 'He's one of *them*,' said a soldier pointing at the enemy. Then the tall, big, tough-looking man called out in a loud, fierce, frightening voice.

'Choose a man to fight me,' he called. Everyone was quiet. No one said a word. David was very puzzled. 'Well?' he said. 'Why doesn't someone go and fight him?'

No one answered him, so David knew they were all afraid. David was even more puzzled. He couldn't understand *why* the men were afraid. After all, God was with them. There was no reason to be afraid when God was looking after them.

68

'I'll go and fight him,' said David. 'Ooh!' said the soldiers in surprise and went and told the king. 'I'll go and fight him,' said David to the king.

'But you are only a boy,' said the king.

'God has helped me to kill lions and bears,' replied David. 'He will help me to kill this wicked man.'

So David began to walk towards the tall, big, tough-looking man. Everyone was watching. Everyone was quiet. David knelt down by the riverbank. He picked up one, two, three, four, five, round stones.

The wicked man laughed and laughed and laughed when he saw David with his stones. He began to shout rude things, but David only called back. 'God will help me,' he said. 'God will win this battle.'

Then David took one round stone and he put it in his sling. He swung his arm as though he were pretending to be a windmill. One, two, three, whee – ee – ee plomp! went the stone, and thump went the tall, big, tough-looking man flat on the ground.

When the enemy saw this, they all began to run away.

A Prayer

Dear Father God, thank You for being with me and helping me to do difficult things. Amen.

David's best friend

Timothy, Clive, Philip and Paul all played together in the alley behind their brown brick homes, but it was Paul that Clive invited to tea. It was Paul who went with him to the park. It was only Paul who was allowed to play with the new toy garage Uncle John had given Clive for his birthday last week. 'He's my friend,' Clive would tell everyone, 'My *best* friend.'

Grown-ups share things with their best friends, too. David did, and he was grown-up. The name of his best friend was Jonathan. He was a special friend because he was a king's son, a prince. Prince Jonathan had many lovely things. He had elegant coats, shining armour and belts studded with jewels. He had bows and arrows and a special sword. Jonathan wanted to show David how much he liked being his best friend, so he gave him the elegant coat he was wearing. He gave him his shining armour, his belt studded with jewels, some bows and arrows and his own sword. Then David looked very grand indeed.

Sometimes David and Jonathan would go out together. Sometimes they would shoot their bows and arrows together. Sometimes they would just talk to each other like best friends do. Sometimes they both talked about God, because they both liked to obey Him.

Then one day the King, who was Jonathan's father, was in a bad temper. He was always in a bad temper nowadays but today he was worse than ever. He didn't really love God and was growing into a nasty, cruel man. Because everyone else liked David, he didn't. He wanted people to like *him.*

'I must get rid of David,' he said.

'What shall I do?' said David to Prince Jonathan.

'You go and hide,' said Prince Jonathan. 'My father may change his mind when he's not in such a bad temper. I'll try to find out if he really wants to get rid of you.'

'How will you let me know?' asked David.

Jonathan thought for a moment. 'Come out into the fields,' he said. So David went with him. There, they found a heap of stones. It was as tall as David when he stood up, and as wide as David when he lay down.

'Not tomorrow, or the next day, but the day

after that, you come and hide behind these stones,' said Jonathan. 'Then I'll come out here with my bows and arrows and a small boy. I'll put an arrow in my bow and I'll pull the string and I'll shoot high into the air. I'll do it again and then again. Then I'll send the small boy to fetch the arrows. Now, listen David. . . .'

David looked at Jonathan, and listened very carefully indeed.

'I'll call in a loud voice to the small boy. So loud, that you will hear me too.' Jonathan went on. 'If I say "The arrows are *THIS* way" it will be a secret way of telling you to come this way back to the palace because the King won't beat you. If I say "The arrows are

A LONG WAY AWAY,'' it will be a secret way of telling you to go a long way away because the King is still in a bad temper.'

David nodded. Then he and Jonathan said goodbye to each other. Jonathan went back to the King's palace and David went away to hide.

One day went by, and the next, and the day after that came. Carefully David hid behind the tall, wide heap of stones. It wasn't long before he saw Jonathan coming. As he peeped out from behind the stones, he could see the small boy skipping along beside him.

Jonathan took one arrow, put it in his bow, pulled the string and whoo!—it shot high into the air. So did the next arrow, and the next. 'Run and fetch them,' commanded Jonathan. The small boy darted off. 'The arrows are a long way away,' called Jonathan after him. David heard what Jonathan said. He knew he must run a long way away and hide, but he knew that God would take care of him. His best friend, Prince Jonathan, knew that, too.

A Prayer

Dear God, You always took care of David. Please take care of me and my family. Amen.

The King is kind

'We hop, we skip, we jump and run. We chase about and have good fun,' sang the boys and girls. Mephibosheth watched. He couldn't join in and play with them for he was handicapped. His ankles didn't move like the ankles of all the other boys and girls, so he had to go everywhere leaning on two wooden crutches. The boys and girls went on playing. 'We hop, we skip, we jump and run. We chase about and have good fun,' they sang again. Mephibosheth turned. Thomp, thomp, went the wooden crutches as he moved off down the dusty street. Thomp, thomp, thomp. . . .

'If only I could play like they can,' he thought. 'If only I had a Mummy and Daddy like they have,' he thought again. But Mephibosheth couldn't walk, and he didn't have a Mummy and Daddy to care for him and love him.

Mephibosheth grew for as long as it takes to grow up, then he became a man, a lame man who still walked on crutches. He even had a little boy of his own who sang like all the other boys and girls, 'We hop, we skip, we jump and run. We chase about and have good fun,' as he played outside his house.

Then one day a strange man came to the door of the house where Mephibosheth lived. 'The King wishes you to go to his palace,' said the man at the door in an important voice. Of course, Mephibosheth went at once.

'Why does the King want to see me?' he thought. 'Have I done something wrong?' When he reached the royal palace, Mephibosheth was taken to see the King.

'Don't be frightened,' said King David when
he saw him. 'Your Father was Jonathan,
my best friend.'

'God has been very kind to me,' said King David. 'He has given me many fields and hills and rivers and houses and gardens as well as a great deal of money and men to serve me. I promised your father that I would be as kind to you as God has been to me.'

Mephibosheth was amazed. He felt most excited. He felt like dancing or jumping up and down — but, of course, he couldn't, because he was a cripple.

King David called a servant to him.

'Give Mephibosheth everything that belonged to my best friend Jonathan,' he said.

'Give Mephibosheth the fields, the hills, the rivers, the houses and gardens that belonged to my best friend Jonathan,' he said.

'Give Mephibosheth money and servants to look after everything I have given back to him,' he said.

So King David kept the promise he had made to his best friend Jonathan. He was kind to Mephibosheth because God had been kind to him. Now Mephibosheth had fields and hills and rivers and houses and gardens

and money and men to serve him. And every day he had breakfast and lunch and tea and supper in the palace with King David.

A Prayer

Dear God, thank You for being kind to me. Help me to be kind to everyone too, especially . . . (Think of some people you can be kind to.)

A helpful girl

Sarah stood watching Mrs. Naaman. Mrs. Naaman was crying. Sarah had never seen a grown-up cry before. She thought that only boys and girls cried, but Mrs. Naaman had real tears falling down her cheeks.
84

'What is the matter?' asked Sarah.

'Oh, I didn't know you were there,' said Mrs. Naaman. She quickly dried her eyes with her handkerchief and smiled — in the way that grown-ups do when they are trying to be brave in front of children. 'I'm all right,' she said. But Sarah wasn't going to be put off.

'What's the matter?' she asked again.

'Well, it's Mr. Naaman,' Mrs. Naaman replied. 'You see, he is not very well. He's caught leprosy.'

Sarah knew what *that* meant. It was much worse than catching measles or mumps or chicken-pox. Mr. Naaman would get worse and worse and worse, instead of getting better. The doctors wouldn't be able to help him, for there was no medicine he could take to make him better, and no coloured pills that he could suck. Even if he stayed in bed, that would not help him to get well again.

Sarah looked at Mrs. Naaman again. She remembered that *her* mother used to put her arms round her and cuddle her till she stopped crying — but Sarah knew she couldn't do that to Mrs. Naaman.

Then Sarah remembered something else. She remembered the way her mother used to tell her that God was looking after everyone in her family, but Sarah knew that Mrs. Naaman wouldn't like her to talk about God. Mrs. Naaman *never* talked about God and didn't love Him one little bit.

Then Sarah remembered Elisha. Surely *he* would make Mr. Naaman better. She ran up to Mrs. Naaman.

'If only Mr. Naaman would go and see Elisha,' she said, 'he would make him better.'

'Who is Elisha?' asked Mrs. Naaman.

'He is a man who loves our God,' said Sarah. 'He lives in Gilgaltown.' So Mrs. Naaman told Mr. Naaman and Mr. Naaman went to see Elisha in Gilgaltown.

Mr. Naaman expected Elisha to do some magic trick to make him well again, but Elisha was a man who loved God and God had made him very wise. When he heard that Mr. Naaman was coming, he sent him a message. 'Go and wash seven times in the river called Jordan,' he said. 'Then you will be well again.'

When Mr. Naaman heard this, he was cross. This wasn't the magic he expected.

'I know much better rivers than the river Jordan,' he said. 'I can wash in them whenever I want to.' Then off he went in a rage. But, after a while, Mr. Naaman calmed down and

didn't feel so angry. Soon, he decided that after all, he would do what Elisha had said. So Mr. Naaman went down to the river.

In went Mr. Naaman and out again, for the first time. He looked at himself. He did not feel better. He still had leprosy.

In went Mr. Naaman and out again, for the second time. He looked at himself. He did not feel better. He still had leprosy.

In went Mr. Naaman and out again, for the third time.

In went Mr. Naaman and out again, for the fourth time.

In went Mr. Naaman and out again, for the fifth time.

In went Mr. Naaman and out again, for the sixth time.

In went Mr. Naaman and out again, for the seventh time.

Hopefully, he looked at himself. He *felt* better. He *looked* better. He *WAS* better! The leprosy had all gone. Now he knew how great God was.

How pleased Mrs. Naaman was and how pleased Sarah was, too! Sarah realized that *now* Mr. and Mrs. Naaman knew how great God was. She knew they would talk about Him in their home now.

A Prayer

O God, You are so very great. Help us to talk about You in our house. Amen.